Edith the Envious Elephant
Written and Illustrated by Lori Kaiser

Another great book in the Xavier Series!

Published by Carpe Diem Publishers
17401 Betty Blvd.
Canyon, TX 79015
806-433-6321

www.carpediempublishers.com

© Copyright, 2010 by Carpe Diem Publishers. All Rights Reserved. No portion of this book may be reproduced, stored in a retrieval system, or transmitted, in any form or by any means, electronic, mechanical, photocopying, recording, or otherwise without prior written permission from publisher.
Printed in the United States of America
ISBN 978-0-9845761-3-5

To my sister and best friend, Emily.
I love you. You are a great mom
and I'm so proud of you.

The best trick Edwina had was to stand on a ball;

But without hard work and practice, that won't be her story.

Edwina was nice and not one to gloat,
But Edith would holler,
"You're dumb as a goat!"

Edith didn't really want to be mean;
But that sin they call "envy"
made her turn green.

She decided to ask Edith, "Hey, girl, what's up?"

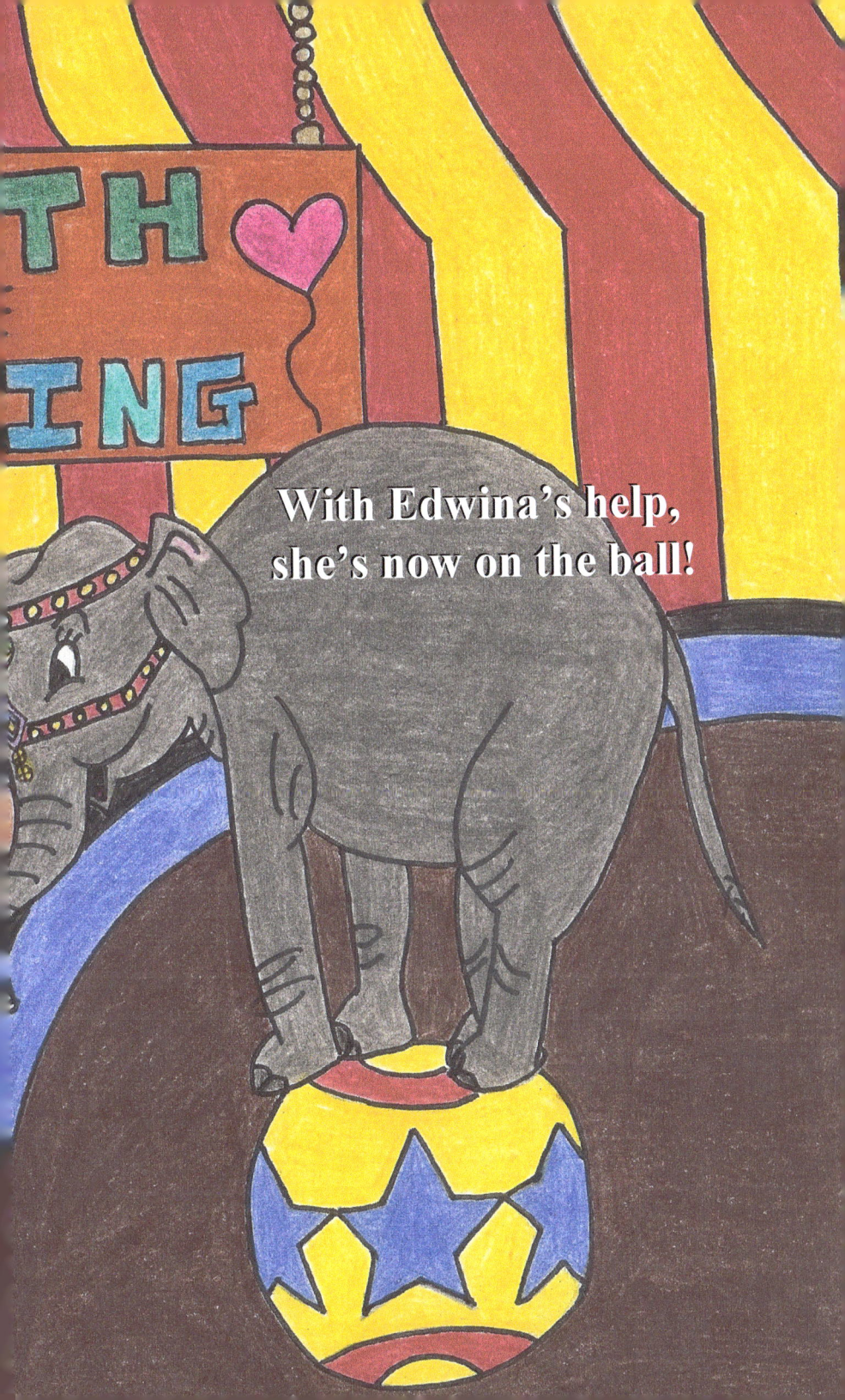

www.ingramcontent.com/pod-product-compliance
Lightning Source LLC
Chambersburg PA
CBHW042045290426